Classic
CARS

A collection of iconic & much-loved classics

Mason Crest

Contents

Mason Crest
450 Parkway Drive, Suite D
Broomall, PA 19008
www.masoncrest.com

©2016 by Mason Crest, an imprint of National Highlights, Inc.

Printed and bound in the United States of America.

10 9 8 7 6 5 4 3 2 1

Cataloging-in-Publication Data on file with the Library of Congress.

Series ISBN: 978-1-4222-3275-0
Hardback ISBN: 978-1-4222-3278-1
ebook ISBN: 978-1-4222-8516-9

Written by: Devon Bailey

Images courtesy of Magic Car Pics, Shutterstock and Wiki Commons

Aston Martin DB5

The Aston Martin DB5 is famous for being one of the most recognisable cars to star in the James Bond series of films. It was featured in several adventures including *Goldfinger* (1964), *Thunderball* (1965), *GoldenEye* (1995), *Tomorrow Never Dies* (1997) and *Casino Royale* (2006). The DB series was named after David Brown, the owner of Aston Martin from 1947-72.

The DB5 was first introduced in 1963 and remained in production until September 1965. It was a more refined and improved version of the DB4 and was arguably the most stylish of all the DB series. Boasting a new aerodynamic front end, standard headlamp cowls and miniature rear fins accentuating the lithe lines of the coupe bodywork, it was a beautifully designed car. It was available as a convertible or sports saloon and included carpets, reclining seats, a fire extinguisher and electric windows as standard. A detachable steel hardtop was optional for the convertible.

Even though it weighed 1,502kg, the DB5 could achieve 0-60mph in 7.1 seconds. Eventually a five-speed gearbox was fitted as standard, producing 282bhp. The Vantage model of the DB5 was of a higher performance with a power output of 325bhp. Launched in September 1963, only 65 DB5 Vantage coupes were ever produced. As well as the Vantage, a number of DB5 convertibles were made. A total of 123 of these were produced, with only 19 being fitted with left-hand drive.

After one year in production, the DB5 was immortalised on the silver screen by Sean Connery in his role of James Bond in *Goldfinger*. The film used the original DB5 prototype and another standard DB5 model for stunts. Ian Fleming had originally placed Bond in a DB Mark III in his book, but as the DB5 was the latest Aston Martin model to be released at that time it was chosen for the film.

The DB5 was replaced in 1965 by the DB6 which was the first four-seater to be produced by Aston Martin.

If you dream of owning a DB5 today, you'll need somewhere near $325,000 to achieve your ambition.

Aston Martin Vanquish

The Vanquish was Aston Martin's pride and joy when launched in 2001 and right up to when production ceased. Designed by Ian Callum it became very widely known following its choice as the Bond car in *Die Another Day* driven by Pierce Brosnan as Bond and has more recently appeared in the *Twilight* film franchise.

It became the must have prestige sports model with its aspirational good looks and brand association. Following its launch in 2001 the S model was introduced with changes including an increase in power from 460 to 520bhp. Other notable changes included the addition of the Vanquish S badge appearing on the boot lid as well as a variation in the nose shape, wheels and brake lights. Sportier features from a 2004 option package were also added.

The model ceased production in 2007, which sadly also saw the closure of the Aston Martin factory in Newport Pagnell and was replaced by the DBS. With the decision to end the production of the Vanquish came the celebratory Vanquish S Ultimate Edition. The key feature of this model was that all 40 cars would have an exterior colour of 'Ultimate Black' along with other individual touches. Unlike previous models the Ultimate Edition was offered with a manual gearbox following much criticism in the motoring press in particular by Jeremy Clarkson.

In the Vanquish's early development Cosworth Technologies had initially been involved in the manufacture of its engine but they had no direct involvement in its design. Ford Research in the USA in fact eventually designed the V12 engine. One of the most technically complex cars that has been built to date the Vanquish continues to be seen on roads across the world with its value somewhere between £40-£50,000 in the used car market for some of the earlier editions.

The Vanquish was based on two concept cars: the Zagato Roadster and the Bertone Jet 2.

Audi Quattro

The Audi Quattro was unveiled at the Geneva Motor Show on 3 March 1980. Styled by British designer Martin Smith, the Quattro set out to rival the likes of the Ford Capri and Opel Manta, both of which were very popular in Europe. It was built as both a road and rally car by the German manufacturer

Audi, which is now part of Volkswagen. The Quattro was the first rally car to use a four-wheel drive system in competitive racing. With this in place, the Quattro won competition after competition for a number of years.

The Quattro was released to European customers in 1980.

Throughout its 11-year production span, 11,452 were built before it was discontinued in 1991. The Quattro had a 5-cylinder turbocharged engine that could achieve 0-60mph within 7.1 seconds. It was not until 1982 that right-hand drive Quattros began to appear. The following year the Quattro's early twin-headlamps were phased out in favour of sleeker single units.

Audi had released a small number of Quattro Sport models

in 1984 but the design was far from appealing. Its shorter wheelbase gave it an odd appearance while its huge rear wing, large wheel arches and bumper free nose made it look even more ungainly. Each car cost £51,000 and proved to be the most desirable and collectable of all the Quattro models. Only 200 Quattro Sports were ever produced, 20 of which were brought to the UK.

In 1985, the Quattro design was again revised slightly, seeing the engine capacity expand with a smaller electronic controlled turbocharger fitted to help eliminate any turbo lag. A Torsen differential was fitted which helped increase the car's grip, preserving Audi's superiority over their rival manufacturers.

With the Quattro nearing the end of its production in 1989 Audi produced the Quattro 20V. As the name suggests, it had a 20-valve cylinder head, boosting the power to 220bhp. It had a much more luxurious interior than its previous models and remained the main Quattro model until late 1991.

DCI Gene Hunt (played by Philip Glenister) drove a red 1983 Quattro in the BBC television drama Ashes to Ashes.

Bentley 3-Litre

The Bentley 3-litre was the sports car that announced Bentley as a global automotive power. Weighing just over 1,700kg, it was quite a large car for its time but its innovative technology and strength more than made up for this. "The fastest lorry in the world" is how Ettore Bugatti described the 3-litre. Even so, it went on to win the 24 Hours of Le Mans five times, between 1924 and 1930 in its various forms. Bugatti's comments might have been out of envy due to the fact Bentley had crushed his hopes of winning at Le Mans for many years.

The 3-litre was first seen at the 1919 Olympia Motor Show in London and was put into production two years later. It was to be the first of a legendary pedigree of British sports cars. With endurance racing in mind, owner Walter Owen Bentley designed it to be immensely strong, reliable and enduring. Its mechanical simplicity reduced the risk of failure allowing Bentley to offer an unprecedented five-year warranty on his cars.

Bentley employed some very sophisticated technologies which were previously unheard of in the automotive industry. Things like aluminium pistons, an overhead camshaft driving four valves per cylinder, twin spark plugs and duel carburettors. The 3-litre developed a lot of torque at low revs, which caused less stress on the engine. These features meant the 3-litre

could reach speeds of 80mph, with later models exceeding 90mph.

In 1924, the 3-litre won Le Mans for the first time, putting the British company on the motor racing map. The only retirements from this famous race were in 1925 and 1926, which caused Bentley to develop the more powerful 4.5-litre version. For the next four years running, the 3-litre took victories at Le Mans from 1927 to 1930. By now Bentley had become the dominating force in endurance racing. However, even with all its success, Bentley could not avoid bankruptcy and in 1931 was bought by Rolls-Royce.

The Supersports, of which only 18 were built, was capable of exceeding the magic figure of 100mph.

BMW M3

The BMW M3 series is a high-performance version of the BMW 3-series. The first model was based on the 1986 E30 3-series and was most notable as it was mainly marketed as a racing vehicle. BMW wanted to break into the touring car racing market to compete against the likes of Mercedes-Benz. The increase in demand led to the M3 being adapted into a road car. It had a number of upgrades over the standard 3-series including a more powerful and responsive engine, improved handling, better suspension, a more aerodynamic body and multiple interior and exterior accents with the tri-colour "M" emblem, which stood for Motorsport.

The E30 M3 was the first model produced between 1986 and 1992. BMW engineers stripped the standard E30 3-series body to its

BMW had to build 5,000 M3s for retail sale in order to qualify for Touring Car competition.

core and went about creating the now renowned M3 model. Critics were amazed by the car's behaviour on the road, blending everyday usability with an uncompromised driving experience. Only 5,000 E30 M3s were intended for production, but, by 1992, a total of 18,000 had been produced. The E30 M3 won more road races than any other model in history, considered by many as the world's most successful road-race car.

During the 1990s BMW began to update the M3 design, creating the E36 M3, fitting it first with a 3-litre 6-cylinder engine, which produced 286bhp and later replacing it with a more powerful 3.2-litre straight-6 engine producing 321bhp. It may

not have been as successful on the track as its previous model, but it was highly praised for its handling and engine characteristics.

In 2000 the next generation of M3 was emerging. Sticking with the 3.2-litre straight-6 engine, BMW managed to draw even more power out of the engine. Now the E46 M3 was producing 343bhp and coupled with its advanced suspension and electric driver aids it quickly became a modern day performance icon.

In 2007 BMW released one of the sports cars of our time, the E92 M3. Sporting a massive 4-litre V8 engine, carbon fibre roof and onboard computer, this was the most powerful and advanced M3 model ever made.

Bugatti 41

The Bugatti 41, better known as the Royale, was one of the most expensive luxury cars ever built. Bugatti planned to build 25 of these magnificent cars and sell them to royalty. But, due to the Great Depression, only six were ever made. All six of these still exist today, making the Royale one of the rarest cars in the world.

Ettore Bugatti supposedly designed the Royale after a number of his cars were claimed to be second best to those of Rolls-Royce. The first Royale prototype had a massive 15-litre engine which was capable of producing 300bhp. It was based on an aero-engine design that had been used for the French Air Ministry. The chassis was supported by a conventional leaf spring suspension at the front and forward-facing Bugatti quarter-elliptics at the rear. The large brakes were mechanically operated by cable controls and required a great deal of strength from the driver to operate. The original prototype was unfortunately destroyed in an accident in 1931.

The Royale was in production from 1927 to 1933. King Alfonso of Spain was one of the first to order the Royale in 1928 and was assured by Bugatti himself that his car would be delivered within the year. But the king was left disappointed by the length of time it took to make his Royale and never did receive it. The first Royale to finally reach its customer was not until 1932.

Each Royale would cost the customer a staggering $30,000. Of the six Royales built, only three were sold to external customers, none of whom were royalty, despite that being its original intention. Bugatti himself refused to sell one of these cars to King Zog of Albania after claiming that his table manners were not to his liking.

Everything about the Royale is of the first magnitude. Its size, value and scarcity were all extreme. Each one has a unique body shape, tailored to the original customer's requirements.

Three of the six cars were hidden behind a false brick wall at the home of the Bugatti family to avoid being commandeered by the Nazis during World War II.

Chevrolet Corvette

The Chevrolet Corvette was designed by Harley J Earl in late 1951. Chevrolet is an American division at General Motors and helped produce six generations of Corvette in coupe, convertible, t-top coupe and targa coupe body styles. The Corvette was originally built in Flint, Michigan and St Louis, Missouri before General Motors moved its assembly plant to Bowling Green, Kentucky. In 2003, the Corvette celebrated its 50th anniversary and is the only American sports car ever to do so.

The first Corvette was displayed at the New York Auto Show in 1953. The name was taken from a type of fast patrol ship used by the British Navy. Ed Cole, the chief engineer at Chevrolet, was so enthusiastic about the car that he gave permission to start production even before it had been seen at the Auto Show.

In June 1953, the first Corvette was sold. Only 300 were produced that year, all in the colour polo white. In 1954 more colours were made available, but the Corvette did not sell very well as its performance failed to live up to its stylish looks. A new small-block V8 engine was introduced in 1955, which produced 196bhp. Unlike older Corvettes, this model could do 0-60mph in 8.6 seconds. General Motors only produced 700 of these cars, as there were so many left over from previous years.

In 1956, the Corvette had a new design, boasting a chrome grille, new body, scalloped flanks and a rounded trunk. Finally the Corvette style had been born.

The Corvette changed a number of times over the years and soon became the leading American sports car. During the 1970s, the oil crisis bought about higher fuel prices and a public desire for more economical cars. Corvette continued to produce their beautifully designed cars but gradually lowered the engine's power. This was set to continue until early 2000. The modern engines of today allowed engineers to get a great deal more horsepower out of their engines without wasting unnecessary fuel.

There is a museum dedicated to the Corvette in Kentucky, USA.

Citroën 2CV

The Citroën 2CV was first produced in 1948 and was technically advanced and innovative for its time, making it one of Citroën's most iconic cars. It was in production for 42 years until being phased out in 1990. During this time just over 3.8 million 2CVs were produced as well as a number of variants, which pushed the total to around 8.7 million vehicles made.

During the 1930s, Citroën were designing a car for the people, much like the Volkswagen Beetle of the same era. The 2CV proved to be a more practical, cheaper and robust car than its German rival. Targeted at the majority of the French population, i.e. workers and farmers, it was aimed at those who previously could not afford a car.

World War II caused Citroën to destroy or hide most of their prototype 2CVs while their country was occupied by German forces. These did not emerge again until the war was over and entered production in 1948. By now the 2CV model was 10 years old but this did not mean it was outdated. Customers found it to be an outstanding little car, with its advanced front-wheel drive system and spacious cabin. The 2CV used a horizontal coil spring suspension, which stabilised the car perfectly, allowing it to drive over bumpy roads and even traverse fields with ease.

Apart from a number of engine and interior changes, the 2CV design remained almost identical for 40 years. The majority of 2CVs were sold in Europe, but they never managed to match the success of the Volkswagen Beetle, as it had not been sold globally. Being labelled as a cheap farmer's car meant it had no market potential in more wealthy countries like America. But, the 2CV was actually more advanced than the Beetle and showed that Citroën was emerging as a leading manufacturer for both cheap and expensive cars. The 2CV became such a success that Citroën had to open factories in the United Kingdom, Spain and Portugal to cope with the increasing European demand.

2CV literally means "two tax horsepower" in French.

Citroën DS

The Citroën DS was first unveiled at the Paris Motor Show in October 1955. Styled by Italian designer Flaminio Bertoni, Citroën received nearly 12,000 orders for the car by the end of the show. The DS was produced between 1955 and 1975, selling almost 1.5 million models over this time.

The DS proved to be a symbol of French ingenuity and defied most of the automotive designs of the time. Many people seemed to believe it came from another planet, due to its looks, hydraulic suspension and dashboard layout.

A number of different versions of the DS were introduced during the early years of its production. The ID was a stripped out version, which was introduced in October 1956. It had, no power steering, power braking or semi-automatic hydraulic gearbox. Two years later, in 1958, Citroën released the Break (Station Wagon). Its extended chassis created more room inside, allowing up to seven people to sit comfortably.

A number of companies also worked on creating various styling changes for the DS. The most famous of these was the French automotive coachbuilder Henri Chapron. He started by building one-off conversions before being asked to help build the factory cabriolets as well as a number of special orders for luxury DSs.

The DS helped push the Citroën brand to a whole new level of success. It caused such a big sensation that no new models were introduced from 1955 until 1970. Citroën was unsure whether they could maintain the same bold standard in their future models.

The DS remained popular throughout its production run. However, at the beginning of the 1970s it was starting to show its age and began to seem a little old fashioned. The DS was finally phased out in late 1975 and was replaced by the CX range of family and executive cars. Despite this, the DS still held a beloved place in French society and on 9 October 2005, Citroën celebrated the cars 50th anniversary by driving 1,600 DSs in procession past the Arc de Triomphe.

Should the situation ever necessitate it, a DS can safely be driven on three wheels.

DeLorean

John DeLorean formed the DeLorean Motor Company (DMC) in 1975 but it proved to be a very short-lived manufacturer known for the one model it produced which was the DMC-12 sports car. This model featured iconic gull-wing doors and became famous after it featured in all three of the *Back To The Future* films. DeLorean went bankrupt in 1982, ceasing to exist before the first film was even made in 1985.

Originally based in Detroit, Michigan, John DeLorean had a vision of creating a sports car that had futuristic elements. Most sports cars of the time were very small and compact, making it difficult for larger people to sit inside comfortably. As John DeLorean was quite a tall man, he set out to design a sports car that could accommodate him easily. This is one of the reasons why the DMC-12 had plenty of room inside.

Production of the first DMC-12 was due to start in 1979, but after a number of problems and delays it was pushed back until 1981. When production eventually began, the American market responded extremely well. Over 9,000 DMC-12s – with their distinctive brushed stainless steel bodywork – were sold between January 1981 and December 1982. Even with this promising start, John DeLorean was having trouble funding the company. In late 1982 plans were announced to shut down the DeLorean production line.

Many original DMC-12s have become collector's items and are widely sought after today. Some motor companies were determined to keep the DMC-12 history alive and started up businesses restoring these classic cars. Many people still love researching the vehicle and attending live motor events that have the DMC-12 on show. A large number of these cars are still on the road after almost 28 years; out of the 9,000 cars that were built, it is estimated that over 6,000 are still driving today.

In August 2007, it was announced that the DMC-12 could go back into production after a large amount of public demand. Businessman Stephen Wynne bought all the remaining parts for the car and hoped to begin rebuilding them again in Houston.

Only 8,583 DeLoreans were manufactured between 1981 and 1983.

Dodge Viper

The Dodge Viper is a V10-powered, two-seater sports car made by the Dodge division of Chrysler. It is the single biggest rival of the Chevrolet Corvette, made to be the typical American sports car after taking inspiration from the AC Cobra.

The Viper was initially designed in 1988 and was first seen as a concept car at the North American International Auto Show. Even though this early design was made out of sheet metal, the public reaction was very enthusiastic. Chief engineer Roy Sjoberg was directed to develop it into a standard production vehicle and a team of 85 engineers were assembled to build and develop the Viper design. After approval from Chrysler chairman Lee Iacocca, the Viper was put into production and was finally ready for sale in January 1992. The first generation of Viper was introduced in 1991 and bore the name RT/10 Roadster. Its powerful V10 engine produced around 400bhp.

This two-seater sports car was considered the most influential car Dodge had ever manufactured. The Viper was first introduced in 1992 at the New Mack Assembly Plant. Later the home of Dodge was moved to the Connor Avenue Assembly in October 1995.

The second generation Viper was made between 1996 and 2000. Known as the RG/10 GTS it had a more powerful engine, improved suspension and better set of brakes. The RG/10 GTS, like its predecessor, was chosen as the pace car for the 1996 Indianapolis 500.

The third generation Viper was launched in 2003 and featured some major changes. An innovative design was made in order to improve the already popular and high quality Viper. This new model, known as the SRT-10, had a much more sharp and angled body.

The fourth generation Viper was a more improved version of the SRT-10. Introduced in 2008, it could produce a massive 600bhp from its newly developed V10 engine. This model ceased production in the summer of 2010 making way for the replacement Viper unveiled in 2012.

There were no Vipers manufactured in 2007, as Chrysler concentrated on selling 2006 models before releasing the fourth generation in 2008.

Ferrari 250

The 250 – built between 1953 and 1964 – proved to be Ferrari's most successful early sports car, and included a series of variants before eventually being replaced by 275 and 330 models.

The 250 was put into production in 1953 and continued into the early part of the 1960s. During this time, Ferraris were all custom built and not mass-produced cars, so production of these vehicles was very slow. Specifications for the 250 also varied; as a result the car's power rating, torque and displacement were all different to other similar models. Most 250s did share the same engine, the Colombo 125 V12. It was a very lightweight engine that had an impressive output of 276bhp.

The first race-ready 250 was the experimental 250 S Berlinetta prototype, which was entered in the 1952 Mille Miglia. Moving on from the success of this, Ferrari launched the 250 MM at the Geneva Motor Show in 1953. The V12 powered 250 MM was replaced by the 4-cylinder 625 TF and 735 S later in 1953. A year later the 250 Monza was produced. Although a frequent racing entrant, the Monza failed to

achieve much success on the track. The 250 Testarossa was one of the most successful Ferrari racing cars in its history. It registered three wins at Le Mans, four at Sebring and two in Buenos Aires. The years between 1963 and 1965 saw the launch of the 250 GTO, 250 P and 250 LM which all had a number of successes on the racing circuit.

The 250 design was extremely successful on the racetrack as well as the street. The 250 Europa GT was introduced at the Paris Motor Show in 1954. The 250 based prototype at the 1956 Geneva Motor Show came to be know as the 250 GT Boano. This was a more styled version of the Europa only designed as an exercise by Ferrari. But demand soon called for it to be put into production. The 250 GT Berlinetta, which was also known as the Tour de France (TdF) was sold from 1956 until 1959. Named after the famous bicycle race, 84 Tour de Frances were built. 1957 saw the launch of the 250 GT California Spyder. Designed for the American market, it was Scaglitti's interpretation of an open-top 250 GT. The early 1960s saw a number of modified versions of the California Spyder, Berlinetta

and Coupe Pininfarina produced while the GT Lusso was introduced at the 1962 Paris Motor Show. The car sported flowing lines and a fastback shape very typical of the GT cars of the mid-1960s.

Tractor manufacturer Ferruccio Lamborghini owned three Ferrari 250s but was not satisfied with their performance and comfort so started his own car company in 1963.

Ferrari Testarossa

The Ferrari Testarossa was the successor to the Ferrari Berlinetta Boxer. Manufactured by the legendary Italian giant, this mid-engine sports car was in production between 1984 and 1991. The 512 TR and F512 M were revised models of the Testarossa, which were launched between 1992 and 1996. Between all of these Testarossa models, a total of over 10,000 were produced. The car is known as the Testarossa, meaning "Redhead" in Italian, because of its red-painted engine cam-covers, which were distinctive from the less powerful engine models.

First introduced at the Paris Motor Show in 1984, the Testarossa was the first TR model for almost 30 years. It was technically almost identical to the Berlinetta Boxer although the main changes were to the bodywork; the sharp wedge-shaped nose was removed for a rounder front fascia. The Testarossa's most characteristic feature was the radiator intakes, which were set on each door. This idea would later be adopted by many other mid-engine sports cars.

A Bosch Motronic engine management system controlled the fuel injection and electronic ignition. The cabin of the Testarossa equipped the driver with all the essentials needed and Ferrari even supplied made to measure leather luggage for each customer which was embellished with the prancing horse insignia and fitted snugly in the front of the car. Fitted with its 4.9-litre V12 engine, the Testarossa could reach speeds of 178mph.

The first real evolution of the Testarossa came about in 1991 with the launch of the 512 TR. Its engine was modified in many ways to

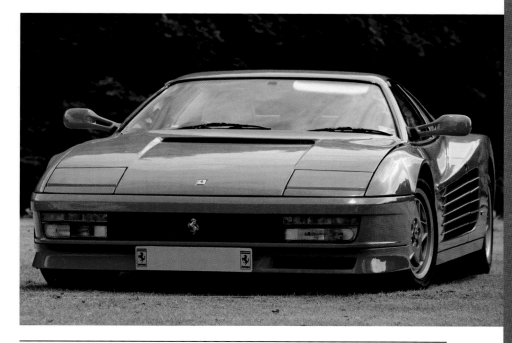

"The Testarossa is unmistakable at any distance, and impossible to ignore." www.topspeed.com

deliver a more broad power curve for better acceleration, enabling it to reach 0-60mph in 4.9 seconds.

Another version was later launched in 1994 in the form of the F512 M (the M standing for Modification). The most notable change was the replacement of the pop-up headlights with the standard body-molded fixed units to save weight.

Fiat 500

The Fiat 500 was designed by Dante Giacosa and was put into production in 1957. Launched as the Nuova 500, it was marketed as a cheap and practical city car. The 500 redefined the term "small car" and it is widely considered one of the first true city cars. In 2007, Fiat launched a modern version of the Fiat Nuova 500, which was similarly styled to the original.

Dante Giacosa, who had previously designed the Fiat 600, which was launched in 1955, wanted to make use of every inch of space in the 500 and so opted for the engine to be fitted in the rear of the car. The 2-cylinder air-cooled unit was a very light design; as much weight as possible had to be shaved off the car for the small 13.5bhp engine to reach its top speed of 52.8mph.

Improvements were made to the 500 in 1958, including an increase in power up to 15bhp. A sport model was also launched with 21.5bhp, which helped keep the tiny car up with the traffic. Fiat continued to improve the 500 models for a number of years, with the main changes being with the engine's overall power.

In 1965 the 500 was redesigned with traditional opening car doors and another boost in power taking it up to 19bhp, giving it a top speed of 59mph. The interior was much more comfortable, with a new steering wheel, instrument panel, reclining seats and carpeting all installed.

In 1972 the Fiat 126 was launched, which was hoped to be the 500's more successful replacement being a more modern version of the 500. It had more power and was slightly bigger and

more comfortable. Despite this, the 126 did not sell as well as the 500 but was popular in the Eastern block countries as it was reliable and had a good fuel economy.

The final series of the 500 was called the 500 R, which was sold between 1972 and 1975, the year in which Fiat stopped producing the 500. During its production lifespan, over 3.6 million were sold.

Fiat previewed a new 500 model in March 2007, exactly 50 years after the first 500 was launched. This was based on the 2004 Fiat Trepiuno concept and proved to be a great success with customers all over the world.

A 1969 Fiat 500 circumnavigated the world in mid-2007 and is believed to be the smallest car to have achieved this feat.

Ford Capri

The Ford Capri was built between 1961 and 1986. A number of different versions were built in the early years of its development including, the Ford Consul Capri and Ford Capri Coupe. At the time the only sporty car available in the UK was the Lotus Cortina and for that reason Ford believed that a new model in the UK would be successful.

The Ford Consul Capri was launched in September 1961 and it was announced that it was for export to Europe and North America only. With increasing demand for such a vehicle it was later released in the UK in January 1962.

The first Ford Capri to use its precise name was not launched until 1969. Debuting at the Brussels Motor Show, with the intent to repeat the same success in the UK that Ford had enjoyed with the Mustang in the United States, the Capri was made to be affordable to

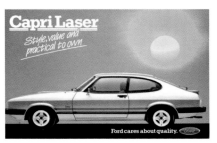

a wide range of prospective buyers, which meant it was also available with a number of engines. By now Ford had started to produce the Capri in an attempt to ensure that every Ford dealer in the country had a Capri in their showroom. Over the next 18 years, two million Capris were sold across Europe and America making it one of the best-selling cars in Britain.

By 1973 despite the fact the Capri had sold over one million units, sales were beginning to drop and the Mk II Capri was soon launched as a more practical, family car. The styling had evolved from the Mk I Capri and the Mk II was slightly longer, wider and taller than

its predecessor and now boasted a hatchback.

The year 1978 saw the final changes made to the Capri design. Extensive changes to the exterior were made to improve the car's aerodynamics for the Mk III. The front of the car was the main focus area in order to reduce drag and improve economy and performance. There were yet more improvements to be made in the following years but the Capri was halted in 1986. There was speculation for many years about the Capri's successor but fans had to wait until the mid-1990s for the launch of the Probe… unfortunately, for Ford, it did not enjoy the same level of success.

Ford Mustang

The Ford Mustang was first manufactured in April 1964 and initial demand for this car was beyond belief. Ford could not make enough as demand exceeded supply by 15 to 1. By 1965 the Mustang had sold just over 680,000, making it the fastest-selling car in history.

The Mustang was available in a wide range of variations from a 6-cylinder to a V8 engine, to a hardtop or convertible. The 260 V8 engine was soon replaced with bigger and bigger V8s over the years.

Carroll Shelby, who also created the Cobra, produced some of the most famous Mustang models. Shelby greatly modified the original Mustang model, increasing the power from 289bhp to 306bhp. The Shelby GT350 was an extremely popular version of the Mustang, with its iconic white and blue stripes.

The second generation of Mustang changed during the 1970s and began to get bigger and heavier but customers were starting to prefer cheaper and more compact cars. The 1974 Mustang was therefore a great deal smaller than any of its predecessors. Based on the Ford Pinto, this smaller, well-trimmed Mustang sold over 385,000 within its first year on sale.

In 1979 the third generation of Mustang was launched. The interior was restyled to comfortably accommodate four people and had a larger engine bay for better service access. The body style included a coupe, hatchback and convertible. Due to increasing fuel prices during the early 1980s, Mustang sales began to drop again. The Mustang model had to develop and a variant of the Mazda MX-6 was proposed. The idea of a Japanese-designed Mustang did not sit well with customers who wrote hundreds of letters of complaint to Ford.

In 1994 the Mustang had a major redesign and was named *Motor Trend* magazine's Car of the Year for the third time. By 2005 the Mustang was updated once again, this time taking inspiration from the original 1960s models. The 2005 Mustang's unique retro look complements its muscle car status.

> *"I told the team that I wanted the car to appeal to women, but I wanted men to desire it, too."*
> Project Design Chief Joe Oros

Ford Model T

Generally regarded as the first affordable car, aimed at the common middle class, over 15 million Models Ts were sold during its production (1908-27), helping to put America and the rest of the world on wheels.

By the time the Model T was introduced by Henry Ford in 1908, Ford was already America's largest automotive manufacturer. The Model T was to revolutionise the motor industry. It had a 4-cylinder

Henry Ford is credited with transforming the car itself from a luxury to a necessity with the Model T.

engine with a detachable cylinder head, which was a new idea for its day. Priced at $850, Ford was under a great deal of pressure to bring this price down. However, Ford refused to compromise the car's quality by cutting costs. The answer came by introducing the world's first moving production line. Each Model T could now be made from start to finish in just over one hour, instead of the 12 hours it previously took. Production increased dramatically and by 1925, the Model T cost only $290.

By 1918, half of all the cars in America were Model Ts. Between 1915 and 1925, all Model Ts were painted black. Ford famously stated, "Any customer can have a car painted any colour that he wants so long as it is black". It is believed Ford chose black during this time because the paint dried faster than other coloured paints of the time. Different colours were available for the Model T between 1908 and 1914 and again in 1926-27.

The Model T had very few design changes over its 19-year run and largely remained the same. They were designed in a range of styles including, coupe, touring, runabout and four-door sedans. The Model T also became a popular racer during the 1920s racing on banked board tracks all over America.

Ford produced an astonishing two million cars each year. When the Model T was eventually phased out in 1927, over 15 million had been sold. It was not until the 1970s that this figure was exceeded by the Volkswagen Beetle.

Ford Thunderbird

The Ford Thunderbird was introduced in 1955 with the intention of competing against the Chevrolet Corvette. It was originally a two-seater until 1958 when it was transformed into a four-seater model, with a more boxy shape and a wide pillar roof. Although two-seater roadsters were very popular during the 1950s, many people wanted a convenience car with more room for passengers and luggage.

The Thunderbird was restyled numerous times during the 1960s. It now had a new body shell, which featured a pointed front nose, modest fins and the traditional rounded lights. The wheelbase was lengthened and the overall car's length was increased by 20 inches. These changes were drastically starting to move away from the Thunderbird's original design.

A new generation of luxury Thunderbirds emerged in 1972. Available as a two-door hardtop, the emphasis was on style and comfort with this new model. This continued throughout the 1970s and, in 1976, the biggest and most luxurious Thunderbird was launched.

The year of 1983 was very important for the Thunderbird, which featured a new aerodynamic look and 3.8-litre V6 engine. Shortly after this the Thunderbird Turbo Coupe was released and received a great deal of attention all over America.

By the 1990s, Ford had dropped the Thunderbird Sport and base Thunderbird models. It was felt by many that 1997 was to be the last year for the Thunderbird; Ford began to remove them from their showrooms all over the country and had a new vision for the year 2000.

In 2002 the all-new Thunderbird was released, which featured a modern take on the original 1955-62 designs. These included porthole windows, a hood scoop, rounded headlights and the Thunderbird's trademark badge.

The Thunderbird, much like the Mustang, is one of America's treasured classic cars. After a great number of changes and updates to the original model, it would be a shame if they were to disappear after all these years in service.

Other names suggested for the Thunderbird included Beaver, Hep Cat, Detroiter, Apache, Hawaiian, Fordette and Ty-Coon.

Hillman Minx

The Minx was a series of family cars produced by Hillman between 1932 and 1970. Over the years there have been countless versions of the Minx as well as various badge-engineered versions, which were sold under the Humber, Singer and Sunbeam associations.

The original Minx was introduced in 1932; made from a pressed steel body on a separate chassis, it had 30bhp, which was powered from its 1185cc engine. Restyled in 1936, the Minx Magnificent was launched. This model had a stiffer chassis and the engine was moved forwards to give passengers more room and comfort in the cabin. The Minx was the final model to be launched in 1938 before the beginning of World War II. This version was visually similar to the Magnificent, but was mechanically different with an improved drivetrain, gearbox, differential and steering box.

After the end of World War II, the Minx was sold again (between 1945 and 1947) and was known as the Minx Mk I. The Minx Mk II was essentially a modified version of the Mk I and was produced between 1947 and 1948. The Mk III was sold from 1948, offering a variety of different body styles including a saloon, estate and convertible version, and produced 35bhp, which was largely unchanged from the previous model.

A number of design facelifts followed, until 1953 when the fourth variation was produced, the Hillman Minx Californian. Over the years the engines had grown from 1390cc to 1725cc in certain models. By 1958 the Minx could reach a top speed of 76mph and achieve 0-60mph in 25.4 seconds. The 1960s saw a number of Minx variants like the Singer Gazelle and Sunbeam Rapier, whose names were derivatives from the later Rootes Arrow range. Models like the Sunbeam and Humber were rebadged and made ready for different international markets. The Minx officially ceased production in 1970 but a number of variations continued to be made by other companies for some years after.

"The new Hillman Minx's low build and attractive lines make it one of the most alluring medium-sized saloons ever built in this country."
The Motor, *May 1956*

Jaguar E-type

An appealing combination of good looks and high performance made the Jaguar E-Type – manufactured between 1961 and 1974 – a motoring icon during the 1960s. Over 70,000 E-Types were made and sold during its time in production.

The first generation E-Type was introduced in March 1961, fitted with the triple carburetted 3.8-litre 6-cylinder engine from the Jaguar XK6. The first 500 cars that were built had flat floors and external hood latches, which made them more rare and valuable. The E-Type had some key distinguishing features including glass covered headlights, signal taillights above the bumpers and its small "mouth" opening at the front of the car. All E-Types featured a fully independent suspension, which improved their ride and handling along with power assisted disc brakes on each wheel, which was uncommon for cars at this time.

The second generation E-Type (produced between 1969 and 1971) had updated brakes, a wrap around rear bumper, repositioned and larger front indicators and a better cooling system helped by an enlarged "mouth" and twin electric fans. New seats were fitted and the dashboard had a whole new look. Critics claimed that this E-Type model had lost its original style but agreed that it was much more comfortable to drive.

The third generation (1971-74) used a new 12-cylinder Jaguar V12 engine, along with new brakes and power steering as standard. It was very recognisable by its aggressive, slightly slanted front grill, flared wheel arches and V12 badge positioned on the car's rear.

The E-type wasn't just fast and beautiful. With its independent rear suspension it handled and drove like no other sports car of the time.

America loved it so much that they bought them by the thousand. No other exported car has done more for Britain's image than the E-Type. This unique combination of qualities means that the E-Type could potentially never go out of fashion and even now next to an Aston Martin or Ferrari, it is still extremely good value for money.

The Jaguar E-Type was ranked first in March 2008 in the Daily Telegraph's *'100 most beautiful cars' of all time.*

Jaguar Mark 2

Based in Coventry, England, the Jaguar Mk 2 succeeded the 1957 Mk 1 from 1959 until 1967. Being loved by both bank managers and bank robbers, the Mk 2 is still one of Jaguar's greatest icons and saloon cars.

The Mk 2 was both a beautiful and fast saloon, capable of reaching speeds well in excess of 100mph and blessed with a quite extraordinary performance. For the standards of the time, the Mk 2 handled very well, but the gearbox and steering were very heavy and hard work for the driver. Inside the car was as much leather and wood as you would normally find in a Rolls-Royce. The Mk 2 was retailed at around £1,400, which was a bargain in the 1960s. It was also becoming a very established racer and had a great deal of success in the European Touring Car Championship.

The Mk 2 had received a renowned reputation as a popular car among criminals and police alike; being able to produce around 210bhp and reaching a top speed of 125mph it was a very fast and powerful machine and was a very popular getaway car during the 1960s as well as being used by the police as a standard patrol car.

The Mk 2 is well known for being driven by television detective Inspector Morse, played by the late John Thaw and in November 2005 the Mk 2 used in the series sold for a total of £100,000.

In September 1967 the Mk 2 was discontinued, being replaced by the Jaguar 240 and 340 models. These were both interim models, which were designed to fill the gap until the introduction of the XJ6 in September 1968. The 340 was immediately discontinued but the 240 continued as a budget model until April 1969. The Mk 2 remains a typical British icon of the 1960s and is still an attractive car, even by today's standards. Since it first went into production in 1959, over 83,000 were produced.

"The Jaguar Mk 2 is the quintessential classic saloon."
www.classicdriver.com

Jaguar XJ6

The Jaguar XJ series was first launched back in 1968. Under the leadership of Sir William Lyons, Jaguar designed a superb luxury saloon car that excelled in every area that mattered to prospective customers: looks, comfort, space and handling. This car proved an instant sales success going on to win numerous awards including Car of the Year with huge demand resulting in lengthy waiting lists. Even 40 years on, it is a car that is very much difficult to fault.

The XJ6 had a superb 6-cylinder engine along with power assisted steering and leather upholstery as standard on the 2.8-litre model, while the 4.2-litre model offered optional air conditioning.

The Series II XJ6 was produced between 1974 and 1979. Initially this model was offered with two wheelbases but at the 1974 London Motor Show, Jaguar announced the withdrawal of the standard wheelbases and instead subsequent saloons all featured an extra four inches of length in the passenger cabin. To meet United States crash safety regulations, this XJ6 had raised front bumpers, complemented by a discreet additional inlet directly below the bumper.

From 1979 to the present day, the XJ6 series has been modified and redesigned on a number of occasions and has served as Jaguar's flagship model for years.

A 1992 XJ6 once featured in a challenge on the popular television programme *Top Gear*. A rival programme, *Fifth Gear* had attempted to make their XJ6 clear a specific distance, so *Top Gear* took up the challenge, the stuntman driving the XJ6, while towing a caravan off a ramp.

The Jaguar XJ6s of today are designed in Jaguar/Land Rover's engineering centres in the Whitley plant in Coventry and at Gaydon in Warwickshire and are produced in Jaguar/Land Rover's plants in Castle Bromwich in Birmingham and Halewood Body and Assembly close to Liverpool.

When the XJ6 was launched, prices ranged from £1,797 for the manual 2.8 to £2,398 for the 4.2-litre de Luxe Automatic.

Jenson Interceptor

The Mk I Interceptor was launched in October 1966 and cost around £5,340. It was designed by Touring of Italy and built by the Italian coachbuilder Vignale. This had a large square-like grille and dropped fibreglass bodywork. It also included the standard Interceptor equipment including power windows, a heated back window and reclining front seats. There were 148 Interceptors built during 1967, 444 during 1968 and 529 during 1969. The Interceptor's huge rear hatch provided ample space for luggage and gave the car its distinctive look. Both the base Interceptor and the four-wheel drive version were 69 inches wide and their height was 53 inches. However, the Mk II was 191 inches long compared to 188 inches of the Mk I.

Another model developed by Harry Ferguson was called the Ferguson Formula also known as the FF. This FF model was rarer than the Interceptor with only two being made in 1966, 24 in 1967, 62 in 1968 and 115 in 1969.

The Mk II Interceptor was first launched in October 1969 and continued to be modified into the 1970s. The FF version of the time also was updated in the same manner. A total of 526 Interceptors were built in 1970 and 742 in 1971 as well as 68 FFs in 1970 and 47 in 1971.

The Mk III Interceptor was launched in late 1971. The standard Mk II equipment was fitted as standard as well as a number of items that were optional extras; the American Interceptors had air conditioning, a radio, power brakes and power steering. Later Mk III models made use of the Interceptor SP engine. The Interceptor SP had a higher performance and was powered by a Chrysler V8 engine, which could produce 385bhp.

Until 1973, the Interceptor SP remained a high performance car. In 1975 and 1976 the Interceptor Mk III coupe and convertible models were launched without any major changes being made to them. In 1976 the Jensen plant closed down and production ceased. Between 1966 and 1976, a total of 6,387 Interceptors and 318 FF models were produced.

A 1976 Jensen Interceptor Series 3 saloon starred in a late-1980s remake of The Saint, *replacing the previous Volvo P1800 and Jaguar XJS.*

Lamborghini Diablo

In 1990, Lamborghini introduced the two-door Diablo as a replacement to its highly popular 1980s icon, the Countach. Designed by Marcello Gandini, who was also responsible for both the Countach and Miura, the Diablo retained many of the same characteristics of these previous models. They included an aggressive, aerodynamic body shape and the gull-wing doors. However, as Lamborghini was under the leadership of Chrysler, these characteristics were toned down slightly to make the car more comfortable and accessible.

The first Diablo model featured a 5.7-litre V12 engine, which could reach 0-60 in 3.9 seconds. It had both front and rear spoilers, more subtle side intake scoops, and sat on rather large 17-inch wheels. The visibility out of the rear and side windows was much better than it had been previously in the Countach.

In 1993 the Diablo was fitted with four-wheel drive, adjustable power steering and variable suspension. This was done in an effort to expand the car's target audience. A roadster version was quickly added, as was an SV sports package that boosted the power to 500bhp and included bigger brakes.

There have been a number of special edition Diablos launched over the years. The Diablo VT was launched and received ABS brakes and an innovative new dashboard designed as a long strip of glass upon which information would be displayed. The Diablo got faster and faster, eventually reaching 530bhp in 1999 with the Diablo ST, before then maxing out at 550bhp in the 2000 Diablo VT. This new Diablo got a complete makeover, with restyled front and rear ends and air intakes.

A limited edition SE30 was produced in 1993 to celebrate Lamborghini's 30th year of production. A total of 2,884 Diablos were produced in its 11-year history. It was discontinued in 2001 as Lamborghini prepared to launch its brand new model, the Murcielago.

The Diablo was the first Lamborghini capable of attaining a top speed in excess of 200mph (320km/h).

Lamborghini Miura

The Lamborghini Miura was only the second car to be made by the Italian manufacturer when it was first launched in 1966. The Miura holds a very special position in motoring history as it is generally regarded as the world's first "supercar".

Marcello Gandini originally designed the Miura, which was viewed by many to be one of the most beautiful cars ever to be created. It had a large, curved windscreen, which rose to a roof that stood only 1.05 metres from the ground. The twin-circular headlamps were sourced from a Fiat 850 Spider, and were used cleverly so that when they were not activated, they recessed flush against the nose to reduce drag and enhance the beauty of the car.

Unsurprisingly, the world went mad for the new mid-engined Lamborghini. Pop stars and playboys alike eagerly snapped up most of the new Miuras even though each one cost four times the price of a Jaguar E-Type. In less than three years, 474 Miura P400s had been built.

In 1969, the Miura P400S was launched with a reinforced chassis and new Pirelli low-profile tyres. The power was increased to 370bhp and its handling was slightly better than the original car while performance remained unchanged.

In 1971, the Miura P400 SV was born, which to many was the best model of them all. The chassis was stiffened again and the engine was boosted by another 15bhp. The transmission was separated from engine sump to improve lubrication under high G-force. The P400 SV was unquestionably the best handling Miura of all the three previous models. A total of 764 Miura's had been produced by 1972 when production was stopped as Lamborghini prepared to launch their latest new model, the Countach.

The Miura kick-started a two-horse supercar race between Lamborghini and Ferrari who have been attempting to get the better of one another for years and it is something that still goes on to this day.

The Miura is credited with beginning the trend for high-performance, two-seater, mid-engined sports cars.

Lincoln Continental

In 1939, Ford's Lincoln division made the first design for the Continental. The vehicle was so popular that it was produced for over 60 years before eventually being discontinued in 2002. It was always applauded for distinctive styling and luxury. The first Continental was developed and designed by chief stylist Eugene Gregorie. It, along with the Town Car, were flagships of the Lincoln brand for decades. The 1939 model through to the 1948 model Continental is widely noted as one of the most beautiful cars ever built.

The Continental was remodelled in 1955, resulting in the Mk II. This version was a unique design with some of the highest quality control ever seen in the motor industry and was one of the most expensive cars in the world, even rivalling Rolls-Royce models at the time.

Elwood Engel completely redesigned the Continental in 1961 and the new model's most recognised trademark was rear-hinged back doors, which were also known as suicide doors. The 1970 Continental was focused once again on style and luxury. With the

460 cubic-inch engine becoming an option in 1977, it was eventually replaced by the 400 cubic-inch small-block as standard. Between 1975 and 1980, the Continental Town Coupe was available alongside the four-door Continental Town Car and Continental Mk V.

By 1999, sales of the Continental had dropped significantly. It had been once again modified and now boasted a more streamlined look with smoother lines, wraparound headlights and a new grille. The V8's output was also increased slightly to 275bhp.

In 2000, safety features to all Continentals were improved, including standard side airbags, along with an emergency boot

release and child seat anchor brackets. The 2002 Continental was the final model to be made by Lincoln. There had been a large shift in the customer marketplace, which meant large, luxury cars, like the Continental were becoming less desirable or practical in these modern days of motoring.

President John F Kennedy was being chauffeured through the streets of Dallas in a 1961 Lincoln Continental when he was assassinated in November 1963.

Land Rover

Land Rover is probably the biggest four-wheel drive brand in the world. Based in Warwickshire, England, it has developed under a succession of owners including British Leyland, British Aerospace, BMW and Ford. Land Rover is now operating as part of the Jaguar Land Rover business, which is owned by

Early Land Rovers were light green in colour due to the surplus of military aircraft cockpit paint after World War II.

Tata Motors of India.

The first Land Rover was designed in 1948 by Maurice Wilks on the island of Anglesey. Wilks was chief designer at the British car company Rover and is said to have been inspired by the American World War II Jeep he had once used on his farm.

The first Land Rover prototype was built on a Jeep chassis and its body constructed from a material called Birmabright, a lightweight proprietary alloy of aluminium and magnesium. The material was used because of the post-war steel shortage and the plentiful supply of post-war aluminium based aircraft. The metal's resistance to corrosion helped build the vehicle's reputation for longevity in the toughest of conditions.

Launched at the Amsterdam Motor Show in April 1948, the Land Rover was a pioneering civilian all-terrain utility vehicle. There was interest in this vehicle as it could be used not only as a car but also as a power source and a small tractor. In the first full year there was a target to sell 5,000 Land Rovers but this number actually reached 8,000 and by 1951 Land Rovers outsold all other vehicles by 2 to 1.

This sturdy vehicle has been used extensively by the military. Over the years many adaptations have been made to these military Land Rovers including, black-out lights, heavy duty suspension, updated brakes, electric suppression of the ignition system, black-out curtains and mouths for special equipment and small arms. The series II models that were used by the British Special Air Service (SAS) were painted pink and used for patrols in the desert. These were known to the military as "Pink Panther".

There have been many new models designed over the years from the first series I, II and III to the more recent models of Land Rover Defender, Freelander 2, Discovery 5, Range Rover and Range Rover Sport. In March 2008 Ford agreed to sell their Jaguar Land Rover operations to Tata Motors who took over the company in June that same year.

Lotus Elan

The Elan was a two-seater roadster first produced by Lotus in 1962. Ron Hickman, who was responsible for the aesthetic looks of the first Lotus Europa, also designed the original Elan. A number of different Elan series were produced between 1965 and 1975 while Lotus gained a certain amount of publicity when Diana Rigg, playing the character Emma Peel, drove an Elan in the television series *The Avengers*.

Introduced as a roadster in 1962, a hardtop and coupe version soon followed within the next few years. The Elan replaced the elegant but very unreliable Lotus Elite. The Elan was the first Lotus to use a folded-steel chassis under a fibreglass body. Styling features included pop-up headlights, a curved windscreen, roll-up windows and slim bumpers. Like other Lotus models of the time it came in both kit and fully assembled form.

By 1967, the Elan 2 was launched which had a longer wheelbase and a set of rear seats. Staying with the traditional Lotus spirit, it was a fast and agile sports car with very elegant lines. Producing 126bhp and reaching a top speed of 120mph, it combined the performance and reliability of the original Elan but could accommodate four people. Less than 1,200 Elan 2s can be seen on the road today, and they are very favourable with collectors all over the world.

By 1975 both Elan versions ceased production after a total of around 17,000 had been built. The Elan became the first commercial success for Lotus due to its clever design and technical sophistication and has been credited as being one of the main inspirations for the highly successful Mazda MX-5 in 1990.

In 1989 Lotus launched the M100 Elan. This two-seater convertible sports car was built and developed with the help of General Motors. Around £35 million was invested in its development; more than any other car in Lotus history. It featured a fibreglass body over a ridged steel chassis, making it very light. Taking influence from its 1960s ancestor, the M100 was similarly built to achieve performance through light weight.

The Elan is credited as being the world's first production car to feature body-moulded bumpers.

Lotus Seven

The Lotus Seven was a simple, lightweight, two-seater sports car produced between 1957 and 1973. Originally designed by Colin Chapman, the Seven was a very successful model, selling over 2,500 units. After Lotus ended the production of the Seven in 1973, Caterham obtained the rights to continue making a car based on the original design. The Seven was based on Chapman's Lotus Mk VI model and was powered by a 40bhp, 1.2-litre Ford side-valve engine.

The first year of the 1960s saw the release of the Series II, which included several modifications from the Series I. Chapman made changes to the front suspension uprights and steering rack. It allowed the repositioning of the rack in front of the wheel line, theoretically providing better cornering. The Series II introduced the use of a fibreglass body, eliminating the costly hand-beaten aluminium. Aesthetically, the Series II had wider, flatter rear fenders, and the line of the nosecone was raised.

The Series III was produced for a single year in 1968. At this time Lotus held a close connection with Ford and they began to work together on certain models. The Series III for example, was modified to utilise several Ford components. The principal change came in the power base with new 1297cc (68bhp) and 1600cc (84bhp) cross flow engines, labelled the 225E, being offered.

The Series IV was designed in just seven months and presented to the public in late 1969. Being built through a mass assembly, it could be distributed to a greater number of dealers. The Series IV was made up of mostly Ford components and small adjustments were made during the design process. Being released between 1970 and 1973, the Series IV was rated very highly through every road test it undertook.

The Seven continued to be produced after 1973 when Caterham began manufacturing it as a kit car but Caterham agreed that their version of the Seven would not be badged as a Lotus. This more modern version is very popular and has been sold in Canada, Australia, South Africa, South America and Japan as well as all over Europe.

There have been around 90 companies across the globe who have built some form of replica of the Lotus Seven over the years.

Maserati Bora

The Maserati Bora was introduced at the 1971 Geneva Motor Show. Shortly after Citroën took a controlling interest in Maserati in 1968 the Bora concept was proposed. Designed by Giorgetto Giugiaro, it was Maserati's first attempt to build a mid-engine super car. Maserati struggled after being bought by De Tomaso in 1975 and the Bora was discontinued in 1978.

The Bora was a very clean and slightly brutal looking car. It had a 4.7-litre V8 engine, which was capable of producing 310bhp and a top speed of 165mph. It drove the rear wheels through a five-speed ZF transaxle, which was also used in

Ford's GT40 endurance racers.

Citroën had taken over Maserati in the mid-1960s and its presence is evident in the Bora's design. The all-wheel disc-brakes system was activated by the French company's unique high-pressure hydraulics. The Bora used a conventional brake pedal rather than Citroën's mushroom-shaped button. All pedals were adjustable to reach and had the tilt/telescope steering wheel, air conditioning and electric windows all fitted as standard.

The Bora was quite a tough car to drive; feeling heavy at times the engine struggled at low revs, offering a modest 5,500rpm. But

the Bora really came alive in the hands of a fast driver making use of its responsive steering and well-supported suspension.

During its production, the Bora had only a few minor design changes. Early versions had the boot lid hinged at the rear but later European models were hinged at the front end. Early models also had retractable rectangular headlight covers that were later rounded off.

In its production run from 1971 until 1978, around 530 Boras were built of which 44 were imported into the UK. The most productive year of Bora production was in 1972 but the instability of the mid-1970s meant that yet another Maserati classic was never fully developed and potentially proved why the Bora, as some claim, was never really seen at its best.

Maserati only manufactured 524 Boras during the car's production run.

McLaren F1

Luggage compartments ran along the sides of the car and a golf bag was included in the available fitted luggage sets.

The McLaren F1 was designed and manufactured by Gordon Murray and McLaren Automotive. Retailing for around £650,000, a total of only 106 of these models were ever produced. It was certainly one of the most significant British sports cars of the 1990s.

After a great deal of success in F1 racing, McLaren set out to build the world's fastest car. Murray originally designed an idea for a three-seater with a central driving position years before the F1 came into existence. The F1 was made from a set of very unique materials such as carbon fibre, titanium and even gold to help keep the car as light as possible – weighing only 1,140kg.

Using a custom built BMW V12 engine, the F1 could produce around 627bhp. The clever design of the F1 included a venturi (a shaped underbody tunnel to channel airflow) that was positioned underneath the car to help glue it to the road. The F1 could reach speeds of 0-60mph in 3.3 seconds.

Out of the 106 F1s that were built, 64 were standard street versions (F1) and 28 were race cars (GTR). The rest were made of up a number of prototypes, tuned and experimental road cars. It took McLaren over three months to build each of these incredible machines.

Even though production stopped on the F1 in 1998, McLaren still maintains an extensive support service for its customers.

McLaren have a number of service centres around the world and have even on occasion flown a specialised technician to customers' cars.

As of 2008, the F1 remained one of the fastest production cars even made. Since then it has been succeeded by the Koenigsegg CCR, Bugatti Veyron and SSC Ultimate Aero TT. However, all of these latest models reached their top speeds through forced induction, meaning the F1 is still the fastest naturally aspiring production car in the world today.

Mercedes 230 SL

The Mercedes 230 SL quickly became very popular in the United States following its arrival in 1963 and this very quickly led to an automatic version being built. At the time, the 230 SL was commonly fitted with a four-speed manual transmission and 2.3-litre 6-cylinder engine. A total of 19,831 230 SL models were built, of which 11,726 were exported.

The 230 SL was almost a perfect match to the earlier Mercedes 190 model. They both had a very similar wheelbase and there was only a 1.5-inch difference in their lengths. The 230 SL included the first automatic transmission ever offered on a sporting Mercedes.

The standard 230 SL could run the standard quarter-mile in just over 17 seconds and reach 100mph in 27 seconds. Demonstrating this speed, it won the prestigious Spa-Sofia-

Liege in 1963 and went on to win a number of different rally events, proving to the world that it was a very rugged machine that could take the rough with the smooth.

The 230 SL styling was conservative, angular and very much related to the D-B Sedans. An interesting new feature was the optional hardtop's roofline curved upward slightly at the sides to increase rigidity and glass area. New features included roll-up windows, fresh-air ventilation and one of the industry's first multi-purpose control stalks for lights and wipers. The standard soft top folded away beneath a hinged cover, and the square styling allowed for considerably more boot space than on previous SL models.

The 250 SL arrived in late 1966 and signalled the death knoll for the 230 SL. The 250 SL remained

in production until 1976 but could not compete with Mercedes' latest offering. After just 12 months and some 5,200 250 SL models sold, that too was replaced, this time by the 280 SL, which was powered by a new bored-out M130 engine with 2778cc and 180bhp.

The designation SL derives from the German Sport Leicht, *or* Sport Light.

MG Midget

The MG Midget was designed as a small but quirky British sports car, which took a great deal of influence from the Austin-Healey Sprite. Produced between 1961 and 1979 the Midget first used a 948cc A-Series engine that produced around 46bhp. One year later its capacity was increased to 1098cc with the power rising to 56bhp. Front disc brakes were also fitted in place of the previous all round drums, to better handle the car's increase in power.

Equipment offered on the Midget model was extremely limited, as MG only intended the car to be an entry-level sports car. As such the Mk I Midget's roof had to be placed over a frame that needed to be constructed by the driver beforehand. Windows and handles were added for the Mk II version, along with the addition of wind up windows. Again the Midget's power was increased, this time to 59bhp. Further changes made for the Mk III, were somewhat more substantial; the engine was replaced by a detuned 1.3-litre Mini Cooper S engine, increasing power for the Midget to 65bhp.

The overall performance of the car was also aided by the addition of a lower gearing ratio than the earlier Midget models. Aesthetically the car was given a new soft-top roof that was permanently fixed to the car, Rostyle wheels came as standard and the previously square rear wheel arch was now rounded off. These changes ensured the Midget was warmly welcomed both by dealers and the reviewing press across the country.

The Midget 1500 was released in 1974 but in order to meet with US federal regulations a number of changes needed to be made. Some of these changes included large rubber bumpers, increased ride height, the addition of a 1493cc engine from the Triumph Spitfire using a Morris Marina gearbox and the rear wheel arches were now squared off again to increase body strength.

The Midget ceased production in December 1979 with a total of 73,899 of the latest version of the Midget being built. The Midget had proved a successful 'little brother' to the MGB and was sorely missed by its fans.

The video for Donovan's Sunshine Superman *saw the folk singer sitting in an MG Midget on the top of a moving car transporter.*

Mini

Produced at Longbridge and Cowley by the British Motor Corporation (BMC), the Mini was a true icon of the 1960s. Sales of larger cars had slumped due to the fuel shortage caused by the 1956 Suez Crisis. Leonard Lord, the head of BMC requested that Sir Alec Issigonis, who was considered a natural for the task, lead a team and design a proper miniature car no longer than 10 feet.

Working with Issigonis, a small team including Jack Daniels who had also worked on the Morris Minor with Issigonis, Chris Kingham, two engineering students and four draughtsmen set about designing this very popular car. By 1957 the original prototype, known as the 'Orange Box' because of its colour, had been built. The Mini had in some ways been considered to be the British equivalent to the German Volkswagen Beetle, which enjoyed a similar popularity in North America.

The two-door Mini that could hold four passengers as well as luggage was demonstrated to the press in April 1959, at a cost of £496. By August of that year several thousand had been produced in preparation for the first sales. Although sales were slow in that first year – only reaching 20,000 – by 1965 one million Mini's had been produced, with 1971 being the best year, recording sales of 318,000.

With such a success, there were a number of updates made to the basic Mini design, which resulted in the Mini Mark II, Clubman and Mark III. Later came the Mini Cooper and Cooper S, which were both sportier versions.

Famous owners of the Classic Mini have included John Lennon, Paul McCartney, George Harrison and Ringo Starr (The Beatles), Clint Eastwood, and Formula One Drivers Stirling Moss, Jackie

The record for most people to fit into a classic Mini at one time is currently 21. The record was set by Malaysian students and two of them were in the boot.

Stewart, Damon Hill and Niki Lauda. Even Prince Charles was seen driving one in his student days. The famous fashion designer of the times, Mary Quant named the mini-skirt after the car.

When production finally ceased in 2000, BMW became the Mini's successor. Designing a new version of the car, known as the "BMW Mini" or "New Mini" it was well received worldwide. On 3 April

2007, the one millionth BMW Mini was produced after six years of production. This was just a single month longer than it took the classic Mini to reach the same total in March 1965.

Morgan

Henry Frederick Stanley Morgan was the founder of the British Morgan Motor Company in 1909. Morgan began his career at the age of 25 when, in 1906, he opened a garage and motor works in Malvern, Worcestershire using investment from his father. Morgan ran his company for 50 years until his death in 1959, when his son Peter took charge.

Morgan began by producing single-seater three-wheeled vehicles, first shown at the Olympia Motor Show in 1910. Having won a gold medal with his single-seater design when entered in the London-Exeter-London Reliability Trial, Morgan's car was shown in the shop window of Harrods after much interest by its managing director of the time. To avoid British tax on cars, these three-wheelers were classed as motorcycles.

In 1932, Morgan risked a change in their design process and opted to include a fourth wheel to their latest model, known initially as the 4/4. Morgan began to struggle through the next decade as their cars were seemingly outdated and not yet established enough in the automotive market.

As sales in the UK declined, the only thing keeping Morgan alive was its exports to America.

Sales to America during the 1950s and 1960s provided the company with its largest market worldwide, taking up to 85 per cent of all its production. However, this ended in the early 1970s after the US imposed new safety and emission regulations. From 1974 until 1992 all Morgans were converted to run on propane as fuel to pass these new regulations. The company continued to grow and struggled through some rather challenging years.

By 2000, the Morgan factories announced a new model was to be produced. The Aero 8 was immediately recognisable as a Morgan and yet it embodies the best of modern technology. It no longer has the "Z" chassis of all of its predecessors; it uses a rigid aluminium monocoque cell construction. With a 4.4-litre BMW V8 engine and a weight of 1,000kg, it has a top speed of 256km/h.

Morgan is now a very well established automotive manufacturer and has produced a number of beautiful and unique looking vehicles over the years. It continues to go from strength to strength and is set for a very bright future in the motor industry.

Production of the Morgan Aeromax (a coupe variation of the Aero 8) was limited to 100 cars, each costing £110,000.

Morris Minor

Work began in 1942 on what would become the Morris Minor (initially known as the Mosquito) with Sir Alec Issigonis leading the design team. Unlike typical motor cars of that era, it used a unitary body construction instead of a separate chassis and also featured an independent front suspension. The final design was produced at the British Motor Corporation plants at Longbridge and Cowley. Although production was delayed because Lord Nuffield the founder of Morris Motors had not favoured this radical new design, it is thought the car's name was changed to appease him.

A vast amount of work had been done on the Morris Minor when suddenly at the last minute Issigonis decided changes were needed in an effort to "get the proportions right". This meant the prototype had to be cut in half lengthways so that another four inches could be added to the width. There had already been a large number of bumpers produced for the original narrower design but rather than have wastage, the bumpers were cut in half and

Lord Nuffield (aka William Morris) hated the car saying it looked like a poached egg and didn't speak to Issignosis for 11 years.

then a four-inch steel fillet was inserted between the two parts.

The two-door design was launched at the Earls Court Motor

Show in 1948 in the small car section and proved to be the star attraction. In 1950, the four-door saloon was introduced and it proved to be a very popular car for the police as throughout the 1960s they were used as Panda cars; it is hard to imagine catching anyone compared with cars of today as the top speed was just 64mph. The Morris Minor could regularly be seen on television in police series such as *Z cars*, a popular programme of the time. The GPO or Royal Mail as we know it today also used them.

A total of 1,368,291 Morris Minors were produced. Being aimed at the family market made it an extremely popular model. As well as the UK, the Morris Minor was produced by the BMC in Sydney, Australia and then also later in Spain, Belgium, Chile, Italy, Portugal, South Africa, Uruguay, Venezuela and Yugoslavia.

Nissan Skyline

The Nissan Skyline was arguably the Japanese manufacturer's best ever production road car. Starting out as a coupe concept by Prince Motors in Japan, the idea was to design a car with similar looks to its rival competitors. The first series Skyline was manufactured in 1957, producing 60bhp and having a rather sporty shape for its time.

In 1963 the second generation of Skyline was launched. This model had a punchy 1.5-litre engine, which produced 70bhp. Nissan began to enter these Skyline models in local races and this soon led to the Nissan Skyline 2000 GT being introduced. In 1968 Nissan bought Prince Motors and began to launch new Skyline models. The first was the Nissan C10, which was released as both a four-door and two-door model. The C10 continued to be updated throughout the 1970s, seeing the C110 and C210 versions released.

In 1981 a rebranded Skyline was released, the R3X known as the R30. It was a typical 1980s car, which was very boxy in design. This model had a 1.6-litre fuel injected engine and the R30 began to do very well on the racetrack. The R31, R32 and R33 Skyline models were released in the years leading up to 1998. Greatly styled and developed from one another, these cars were dominating races all over the world; no one wanted to race against a Japanese supercar at this time. Nissan released the R34 in 1999. This Skyline model had a 2.6-litre inline-6 engine capable of producing 280bhp.

A major turning point came for Nissan when the V35 Skyline was introduced. It changed the typical Skyline characteristics such as the straight-6 engine and turbocharging. Nissan opted for the V6 engine to be used in their future Skyline models. They aimed

The Paul Newman Version R30 was released in 1983 to commemorate the association between Nissan and the actor.

the V35 Skyline at the luxury sport market and it was eventually sold to a number of countries including North America, South Korea, Taiwan and the Middle East.

A world record was set on 11 April 2010 when the biggest ever Nissan Skyline meeting was held at Silverstone in the UK.

Pontiac Firebird

The Pontiac Firebird was built between 1967 and 2002 by the Pontiac division of General Motors. The first generation of Firebird shared a great deal of its body parts and mechanical components with the Chevrolet Camaro. General Motors were aiming to keep costs down and successfully retained the Firebird's identity thanks to the use of a GTO-styled nose and slimmer rear lights. After a number of different engine choices were used between 1967 and 1969, the V8 was favoured for the Firebird, producing 320bhp and reaching a top speed of 114mph.

The second generation Firebird was produced between 1970 and 1981. The elegant shape of the original was replaced with a boxier look and a large number of engines circled through the Firebird during its life span. In 1974, in reaction to the fuel crisis, an inline 6-cylinder was used for a short time. But the Firebird was best suited to the V8 engine, and before long it was introduced again.

The third generation of the Firebird was in production between 1982 and 1992. Like the model before it, the Firebird had a long production run and had been updated once again. This model continued to be an iconic car for the Pontiac range. The new model handled very well and was the first Firebird to be developed using a wind tunnel. There were a number of changes made to the car over its 10 years in production.

The fourth generation was introduced in 1992; this was the last of the Firebird models. The remodelled design wasn't very popular with customers at first. Pontiac had taken much more influence from the Chevrolet Camaro when designing this Firebird. By the end of 2002, Firebird production came to an end. In 2007, a special Firebird 'Burt Reynolds' edition was made to mark the 30th anniversary of the *Smokey and the Bandit* films in which the Firebird had received worldwide recognition.

James Garner drove a gold Firebird Esprit in his role as the title character in the 1970s series The Rockford Files.

Porsche 944

The Porsche 944 was first introduced in 1982 and was a huge success during the 1980s. It was available in several forms including 944, 944 Turbo, 944 S, 944 S2 and the 944 Turbo S. By 1981, Porsche had produced a total of 28,000 944s and together with the earlier 924 and later 968 models, the 944 accounted for one-third of all Porsche's production output in the early 1980s.

The 944 began with a 2.5-litre straight-4 engine. It was largely based on the earlier 924 models but featured a number of changes to its bodywork although the car's interior was originally kept the same as the 924. During 1985 the 944 received a few more updates, which included a new air conditioning system, as well as new dashboard and door panels being fitted. At this time the 944 Turbo – basically a higher performance 944 – model was released. It used a turbocharged and intercooled standard 944 engine, which meant it could produce up to 220bhp.

In 1987, the 944 S (Sport) was introduced – again with a more powerful engine than the standard 944 – which was capable of producing 190bhp. Newer features for the time like dual airbags and anti-lock brakes were fitted to each model. Later the 944 Turbo S was launched in 1988. It could achieve 0-60mph in 5.5 seconds and reach speeds of 101mph, making it the fastest production 4-cylinder car of its time.

The year of 1991 saw the release of the 944 Turbo Cabriolet, which combined the Turbo S's 250bhp engine with a cabriolet body. Around 625 of these models were built with 100 being made in

right-hand drive form for the UK, Japanese, Australian and South African markets. None of these were imported to the United States.

The 944 had its last year of production in 1991 and was replaced by the Porsche 968. Over 113,000 944s had been produced during the car's lifetime.

In 1984, Car And Driver *named the 944 the Best Handling Production Car in America.*

Porsche 911

Butzi" Porsche, son of Ferdinand Porsche, originally designed the 911. After debuting at the Frankfurt Auto Show in 1963, it went into full production one year later. Fitted with a 2-litre, 6-cylinder engine, the 911 produced 130bhp and had a top speed of 130mph.

In 1966, the 911 S (sporting) edition became available in Europe. It was the first 911 to have five-spoke Fuchs alloys and had a very distinctive red painted cooling shroud around the engine. In 1969 the 911 T (touring) and 911 E (einspritzung), German for fuel

injected, became available.

The 1970s saw a number of Porsche 911 variations emerge. The 911 Carrera debuted in 1972, which was a lightweight, stripped out version of the 911. It could reach speeds of 149mph and was capable of 0-60mph in just 5.5 seconds. The 911 Turbo, also known as the 930, was launched in 1973 at the Paris Motor Show. This was powered by a 245bhp engine and could

achieve 0-60mph in just under five seconds. Porsche launched the 911 SC or Super Carrera in 1978. It was rumoured during the 1980s that Porsche would be ceasing production of the 911 but this enigmatic icon has survived into the 21st Century.

In 1983, the Porsche 959 – which was still essentially a 911 – debuted at the Frankfurt Motor Show to honour the 911's 20th anniversary. However, it did not catch on until

At full throttle, a 911's engine fan blows 1,400–1,500 litres of cool air over the engine each second.

about 1986 and even then only 337 were ever built. By 1989, the 911 had a complete overhaul; it looked very similar to its predecessors but was fitted with a 3.2-litre engine and a tiptronic transmission, which allowed drivers to choose between automatic and clutchless manual gear shifting.

By 1996 the one millionth Porsche had been produced. The 911s of this new generation had to be cheaper and faster to build if Porsche were to stay in business. The 933 was launched and then replaced by the 996 in 1999. These were both still essentially new versions of the 911. The 996 which was also known as the 911 Carrera went on to become the best-selling 911 of Porsche's history, with over 170,000 being sold worldwide.

Rolls-Royce Corniche

Rolls-Royce – a British manufacturer of luxury automobiles based in Goodwood, West Sussex, England – is the current producer of Rolls-Royce branded automobiles, whose historical production dates back to 1904. Rolls-Royce became the owner of the Bentley Car Company and also dictated the development of Bentley cars and started merging their products. The Corniche was such a production, a merge of Bentley and Rolls-Royce's coupe and convertible versions of the Silver Shadow. Five different styles of Corniche were manufactured between 1971 and 2001. This new generation of two-door vehicles brought instant success, being available both as a coupe and convertible.

The Corniche used the standard Rolls-Royce V8 engine, an aluminium-silicon alloy block and aluminium cylinder heads with cast iron wet cylinder liners. The design of the Corniche was thought to make it greater then previous Rolls-Royce models as it was fitted with a hydraulic self-levelling system and a four-wheel independent suspension with coil springs on all four wheels.

Simply the best motor car in the world.

Sir Henry Royce's first job was as a newspaper delivery boy for W H Smith & Son Ltd.

Each of the five Corniche models were devised around the same design but slight adjustments were made to each. Mildly reworked in 1986 as the Corniche II, alloy and rubber bumpers replaced earlier chrome ones. An aluminium radiator was substituted and an oil cooler was added. Other changes included new style rims, a new reverse warning lens type and pattern around the rear licence plate, as well as newly designed seats and a redesigned dash.

The only significant change from the Corniche II to the Corniche III in 1989 was that airbags were fitted as standard. The bumpers were now painted body colour rather than black, and a more advanced suspension system was fitted. In 1993, the Corniche IV made an appearance with a glass rear window, a major upgrade from the old plastic one.

The final rework of the Corniche made its debut in January 2000. At the time of its release, it was the most expensive vehicle offered by Rolls-Royce with a base price of £240,000. Its production was ceased shortly thereafter, in 2001, as Bentley and Rolls-Royce became two separate companies again.

53

Which Rolls-Royce belongs to a man who thought he would never have one?

Rolls-Royce Silver Ghost

In 1906 the Managing Director of Rolls-Royce, Mr Claude Johnson, ordered for a car to be used as a demonstration to raise public awareness of the new company. This resulted in the production of the Silver Ghost, named to emphasise its ghost-like quietness. This quietness was exactly what Henry Royce had in mind when designing this car, as he wanted to replace his rough running 6-cylinder with something more reliable, smoother and quieter. He achieved this by fitting it with a massive, seven-main-bearing crankshaft and stiff crankcase. Its cylinders were cast in two blocks of three, inclusive of heads, which eliminated head gaskets.

Cars of this time were notoriously unreliable and roads of the day could be horrendous, nevertheless, the Silver Ghost set off on trials and, with members of the press aboard, it broke record after record, such as a 15,000-mile trial in 1907, observed by the Royal Automobile Club. Four years later, on the London-Edinburgh-London run, a Silver Ghost ran the entire distance in top gear with a fuel consumption of 19mpg, an astonishing performance for the time in such a heavy car. Although the 7-litre side-valve engine's compression ratio was only 2:1, it developed 45bhp and would deliver 50mph cruising speeds, which was more than any keen driver of that day could do on almost any public road.

The Silver Ghost became the longest-running single model next to the Model T Ford (and, much later, the VW Beetle and the Mini) and is thought to be the most famous luxury car in history. The Silver Ghost was the reason Rolls-Royce were considered to make the "best car in the world". This claim was not announced by themselves, but by the publication *Autocar* in 1907. This may be a key reason as to why it is still to this day the most desirable model among antique car enthusiasts. However you will need a small fortune to be an owner of a Silver Ghost as it is considered the most valuable car in the world; today it is valued at around £39 million.

More than 60 per cent of all Rolls-Royce cars ever built are still roadworthy.

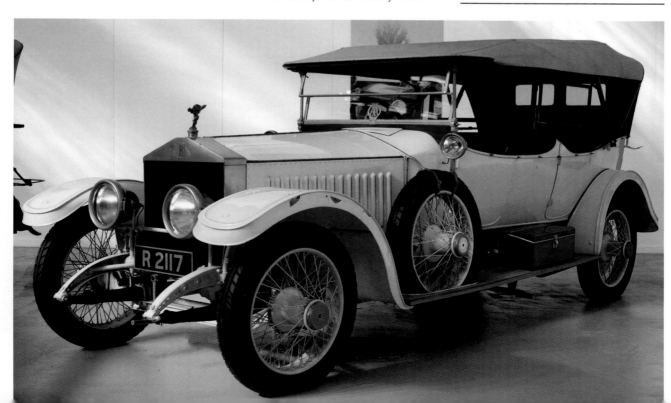

Saab 900

The Saab 900 was a model that spanned the entire 1980s being in production for some 15 years. During its lifetime over 900,000 units were produced by Saab in two generations. The first generation from 1978 until 1993 is known as the "classic" and the generation from 1994-98 is described as the "new generation".

The "classic" Saab 900 is based on the Saab 99 chassis, though with a longer front end. The Saab 900 was a front-engined, front-wheel drive compact car with a longitudinally mounted 4-cylinder engine, double wishbone front suspension and beam-axle rear suspension. There were several available versions: the GL had the single-carb 99hp/73.5kW engine; the GLS had twin carburettors for 106hp/79.5kW; the EMS and GLE had fuel injection for 116hp/87kW; and the 900 Turbo produced 143hp/107kW. The 900 convertible was introduced in September 1994.

Engines were either 2.0 or 2.3-litre 4-cylinder or the Vauxhall-made 2.5-litre V6. Due to the Saab's special engine balance shafts (a 16-valve cylinder head with double overhead camshafts), the 900 was more powerful and a smoother drive. Few adjustments were made to the "new generation" model including colour-coded bumpers being added in 1995 and in 1997 improvements included larger, more supportive front seats with velour upholstery, a more precise gear change, larger brake discs and heat-reflecting glass. However the 1998 year-model cars underwent some greater changes, with the main one being the dropping of the V6 engine replaced with a choice of three engines consisting of 2.0i (130bhp), 2.0T (185bhp) and 2.3i (150bhp) petrol installations. The range was added to in June 1998 with the launch of a light-pressure turbocharged version of the 2.0T engine. It developed 154bhp and replaced the 2.3i versions. In November 1998 another engine variant was launched, the HOT designation, which was basically a powerful 2.0 turbocharged unit developing 205bhp.

The first generation "classic" 900 is still the best-selling Saab of all time.

Toyota Celica

The Toyota Celica was originally designed for motorists who love fun and style rather than just as a simple means of transportation. The Celica's name is derived from the Latin word *coelica* meaning "heavenly" and is applied to a series of popular coupes made by the Japanese company. The Celica was Toyota's version of the Mustang, which was an image car rather than a high-volume car.

Throughout its lifespan from 1970 until 2006, various 4-cylinder engines have powered the Celica.

In 1974 the GT model was added. The 2T-G that powered the high-end GT model was a DOHC twin-solex carburettor 1600cc engine. The GT model came with various upgrades like underbody spoilers, tinted windows, different hood flutes, power windows, air conditioning and the GT front grill.

The second generation of Celica was released in 1978 and was powered by a 2.2-litre engine. This new model offered more safety, power and economy than previous models, and was awarded *Motor Trend's* "Import Car of the Year" for 1978.

In 1982, the third generation of the Celica was launched. The styling was changed considerably from previous models and its power was now provided by a 2.4-litre engine. The most significant change, however, occurred with the fourth generation, in August 1985, when the car's drive layout was changed from rear-wheel drive to front-wheel drive. The four-wheel drive turbocharged model was produced between 1986 and 1999.

The fifth generation Celica was introduced in September 1989 receiving revised styling, upgraded wheels, tyres, and more power. The sixth (1994-99) and seventh (2000-06) generation main changes were seen in the style of each car; models have been revised many a time, available as notchback and liftback coupes, as well as a convertible.

The very first entry for the Toyota Celica in the World Rally Championship was in the 1972 RAC Rally, when Ove Andersson drove a TA22 1600GTV into ninth place.

Toyota MR2

The MR2 was a small, two-seater sports car first produced in 1984. Toyota set out to build a car that was very enjoyable to drive and had a sufficient fuel economy. The initial designs were not meant for a sports car, but after a number of successful prototypes, that is exactly what the MR2 evolved into. Toyota made three different generations of MR2 before production stopped in Japan during July 2007. The name MR2 is defined by Toyota as meaning "Mid engine, Runabout, 2-seater." But most owners now prefer the explanation to be "Mid engine, Rear drive, 2-seater."

The first generation MR2 was produced between 1984 and 1989 at a time when Lotus and Toyota were closely co-operating with one another and both companies worked together on a variety of designs and prototypes. There were rumours that Lotus was heavily involved with the original MR2 design but it is believed that the MR2 was designed by Toyota but under the supervision of Lotus

engineer Roger Becker. The car that was produced had an angular, origami-like set of lines giving the car its unique look. The most powerful engine of this model was capable of 145bhp.

The second generation MR2 was produced between 1990 and 1999. This model was slightly larger than the first and had a more graceful body shape which some compare to the Ferrari sports cars of the time. It was more powerful but slightly heavier than the first model with the top engine producing 240bhp. The majority of these MR2 models were hand built by Toyota.

Toyota shortened the MR2's name to MR in France because of the similarity to a common French swear word.

The third generation MR2 was produced between 2000 and 2007. This model took a great deal of inspiration from the Porsche Boxster and Lotus Elise. It was a lightweight car that produced only 138bhp but proved very quick and nimble on the road. Toyota opted for this to be a more stripped out model with the focus on handling rather than straight-line speed. This was clearly a car that was built to be enjoyed being driven.

Triumph Herald

The Triumph Herald was built in Canley, Coventry with the aim of replacing the Triumph Standard 8 and 10 models. Designed by Giovanni Michelotti, this exciting small two-door car was unveiled for the first time at the Royal Albert Hall in 1959.

With its clean interior, modern lines and large glass windows providing a great deal of visibility, it was a very practical little car. The Herald was fitted with a single speedometer, situated in front of the driver with built-in fuel gauge, carpets and a heater supplied as standard although there were options of leather seats and a wood veneer dashboard trim. Although received well by the press and dealers at a cost of £700 it had to compete with more successful cars of the time such as the Morris Minor, Ford Popular and Austin A35 which were less well-equipped but more

affordable for most families. Also its performance proved average reaching 60mph in a very timely 31 seconds. However with its excellent visibility, incredible turning circle and light steering the Herald proved to be a very popular vehicle with driving schools.

With the takeover of Triumph in the early 1960s by British Leyland more resources soon became available. In 1961 the Triumph Herald 1200 was produced boasting a larger engine, new bumpers and an overall improved interior.

The Herald was transported all around the globe with sales of over 300,000 and was indeed a success

for Triumph as its chassis was used many times as the basis for other cars produced by Triumph like the Vitesse, GT6 and Spitfire.

Today a good number of Heralds still survive in the UK and there is a great deal of support shown by enthusiasts for these little cars. On BBC One's show *Top Gear*, presenter James May has twice used a Herald as an amphibious car: firstly in a challenge to cross a two mile lake and then in an attempt to cross the English Channel. Now this battered Herald model rests as part of the scenery at the *Top Gear* studios.

The first model to go on sale was the Coupe, not necessarily a four-seater car as the rear seat was optional.

Triumph TR7

programme, actress Joanna Lumley who played the character Purdey often drove the yellow Bullet.

Early in 1979, Triumph produced the TR7 Drophead, a convertible version that again went on sale in America. This convertible was designed by Michelotti and later went on sale in the UK in 1980 at a cost of £5,050.

From 1976 to 1980 British Leyland ran a number of TR7s in rally competitions and although not performing so well off road they were reasonably successful when competing on tarmac.

Concerns were voiced when at the Frankfurt Motor Show in September 1977 a press car developed overheating problems when it was run at maximum speed. By 1981, as part of a rationalisation by British Leyland boss, Michael Edwardes, all TR7 production was finally halted.

The Triumph TR7 was designed by Harris Mann and manufactured by the Triumph Motor Company, a part of British Leyland in the Liverpool factory at Speke from September 1974. It was later produced at Canley, Coventry and then in 1980 at the Rover plant in Solihull. During its production the car was referred to as the Bullet, from the saying "it goes like a bullet" and this phrase was used in various adverts showing the TR7. Although produced in the UK, the TR7 was first launched in 1975 in America. Due to the high demand for this model, the launch in the UK had to be delayed until May 1976.

The two-door TR7 was characterised by its wedge-shape and had a distinctive curved line in the bodywork from the door to the rear of the car. Powered by an 8-valve 4-cylinder engine which shared the same basic design as the Triumph Dolomite Sprint, it could produce up to 105bhp reaching a top speed of 109mph. This spacious two-seater outsold all other TR models at that time.

On television during the late 1970s, a yellow hardtop TR7 could regularly be seen in a series called *The New Avengers*. In the

The TR7's handling was likened to that of a Lotus but build quality was questionable.

TVR

TVR is a British sports cars manufacturer that until 2006 was based in Blackpool, Lancashire where its former owner Trevor Wilkinson was born on 14 May 1923. Since 2006 the company has split into several subsidiaries which are now located in other areas across the UK. TVR's name is taken from the same letters within its owner's Christian name, Trevor. After leaving school at 14 to attend a local garage to start an engineering apprenticeship in 1946, Wilkinson bought a wheelwright's business and renamed it Trevcar Motors.

By 1947 Wilkinson had built his first car, a special two-seater body on an Alvis Firebird chassis. The TVR engineering company was formed when Wilkinson and his partner Jack Pickard started a separate company. In 1949 Wilkinson and Pickard produced their first car, a two-seater alloy-body on a tubular chassis. The company's name was finally changed to TVR in 1954 when the first production car initially called the Mk I was later named the Grantura. Most TVRs were sold to the British market and to avoid British tax paid on assembled cars they were produced as kit cars. This practice continued until the 1970s when this law was changed.

By 1962 both Wilkinson and Pickard left the company to set up an independent fibreglass and engineering business. TVR changed hands many times, even facing bankruptcy before being bought by Arthur and Martin Lilley in 1965. In 1967 TVR turned to Ford for a V6 engine for their new model the TVR Tuscan. Reaching 0-60mph in 8.3 seconds, it gave a great performance for this time.

Peter Wheeler took ownership of the company in the 1980s and TVR began to move away from the turbocharged V6s and back to larger V8 models like the Rover V8. In the 1990s, TVR modified a number of Rover V8s with the new lightweight AJP8 engine. Wheeler was instrumental in helping the design team produce a number of acclaimed TVR body designs, including the Chimaera, Griffith, Cerbera, Tuscan, Tamora, T350, Typhon and Sagaris.

In July 2004, Nikolay Smolensky bought TVR for an estimated £15 million. By 2006 Smolensky had split TVR into a number of different companies, TVR Motors, TVR Power and Blackpool Automotive. Despite his Russian nationality, Smolensky insisted that TVR remained a British company.

TVR has been described as the last great sports car company.

Vauxhall Viva

The Viva was produced by Vauxhall Motors and was the company's first compact car since World War II. At the time of its launch the Viva's principal competitors were the Ford Anglia and Morris Minor. This new, nippy, lightweight, easy to operate control car with good visibility was one of the first cars to be actively marketed at women drivers.

Between 1963 and 1979 there were three versions produced, known as the HA, HB and HC. A van version of the HA Viva was known as the Bedford Van, these continued to be produced until 1983. During the first 10 months, over 100,000 versions of the Viva model had been sold and by 1966 this figure had reached more than 306,000.

However Vauxhall gained a reputation for producing rust-prone models, though at that time they were not the only manufacturer to suffer. The HA Viva also suffered badly with handling and stability problems. The front steering, suspension and engine mounting assembly proved very popular with DIY hot rod builders in the UK due to its simple mechanics.

In 1966 the HB Viva was announced. Even though it was larger than the HA Viva with a heavier body, it retained the nippy performance and was sold until 1970. The HB Viva used a completely different suspension design, and there were optional front and rear anti-roll bars. Unfortunately problems were later identified on this model as in a survey in 1971 the HB Viva came top as the car most likely to have faulty brakes… of the cars tested in this survey 26 per cent were affected. In Britain in the late 1960s and early 1970s *Motor* magazine polled readers on their cars, and of 1,600 owners of the HB Viva only 21 per cent answered that they would buy another car of the same model.

Throughout the 1970s, Vauxhall produced the HC Viva. This model was mechanically the same but offered greater interior space and came with modern styling. It was also available in Magnum and Firenza versions but became obsolete with the introduction of the Astra in 1979.

"If the Viva lingers in people's affections, it's because it was the 1960s' answer to a trusty steed."
The Independent

Volkswagen Beetle

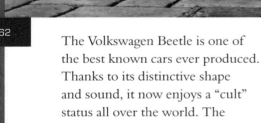

The Volkswagen Beetle is one of the best known cars ever produced. Thanks to its distinctive shape and sound, it now enjoys a "cult" status all over the world. The Beetle was in production from 1938 until 2003 in which time over 21 million cars were produced.

In 1934 Adolf Hitler expressed that he wanted a car to be built that was not just exclusive for the rich. Ferdinand Porsche was put in charge of this operation to develop a Volkswagen (the people's car). By 1936 the first prototypes were ready for testing, with the car being designed to be as simple as possible mechanically so that there was less to go wrong.

Originally referred to as the Volkswagen Type 1, it was not until August 1967 that Volkswagen began using the name "Beetle" in its marketing materials in the United States. The Beetle, with its round shape and air-cooled,

Great shape to be in.

Hitler's criteria included a top speed of 62mph, 42mpg, the ability to transport two adults and three children and a sales price of no more than £86.

rear-mounted engine was seen as the German equivalent to the British Morris Minor.

In the 1950s the Beetle was more powerful and comfortable than most other small European cars,

Nobody's perfect.

after specifically being designed to travel at high speed on the Autobahn. The Beetle proved to be so popular that it was later assembled in Australia, Belgium, Ireland, Brazil and Indonesia.

With its unique appeal, the Beetle was the subject of a Disney film called *The Love Bug* released in 1968. This told the story of a white VW Beetle with the name Herbie who had the ability to drive itself, open and shut its own doors etc. This film proved so popular that sequels were later made and it importantly helped raise the Beetle's worldwide profile.

In an international poll for the world's most influential cars of the 20th Century the Beetle came fourth. In total 21,529,464 Beetles were produced and of those 15,444,858 were made in Germany. Only a handful of Beetles were produced primarily for the use of the Nazi elite in the years 1940-45.

As of 2010, the Beetle is arguably the world's best-selling car design and such was the revere in which it was held that Volkswagen launched the "new" Beetle in 1998 with modern technology but with obvious styling that pointed to its heritage.